COSMOS QUESTIONS
WHAT WAS THE BIG BANG?

by Clara MacCarald

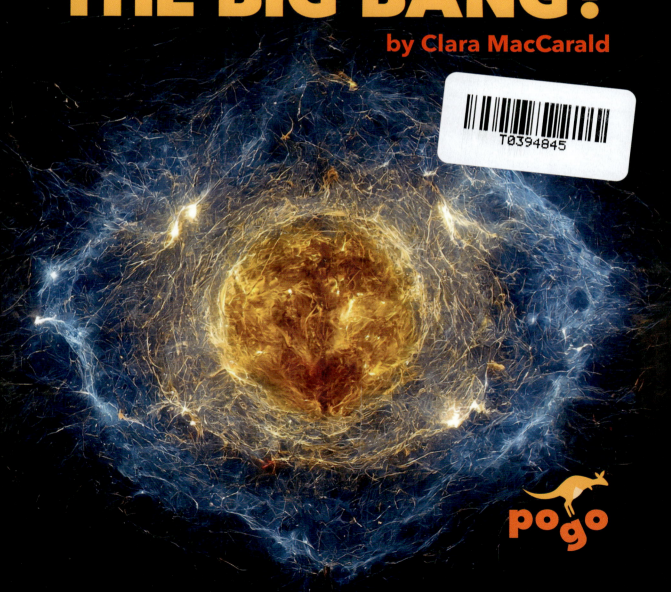

pogo

Ideas for Parents and Teachers

Pogo Books let children practice reading informational text while introducing them to nonfiction features such as headings, labels, sidebars, maps, and diagrams, as well as a table of contents, glossary, and index.

Carefully leveled text with a strong photo match offers early fluent readers the support they need to succeed.

Before Reading

- "Walk" through the book and point out the various nonfiction features. Ask the student what purpose each feature serves.
- Look at the glossary together. Read and discuss the words.

During Reading

- Have the child read the book independently.
- Invite them to list questions that arise from reading.

After Reading

- Discuss the child's questions. Talk about how they might find answers to those questions.
- Prompt the child to think more. Ask: What did you know about the big bang before reading this book? What more would you like to learn?

Pogo Books are published by Jump!
5357 Penn Avenue South
Minneapolis, MN 55419
www.jumplibrary.com

Copyright © 2026 Jump!
International copyright reserved in all countries. No part of this book may be reproduced in any form without written permission from the publisher.

Jump! is a division of FlutterBee Education Group.

Library of Congress Cataloging-in-Publication Data

Names: MacCarald, Clara, 1979- author.
Title: What was the big bang? / by Clara MacCarald.
Description: Minneapolis, MN: Jump!, Inc., [2026]
Series: Cosmos questions | Includes index.
Audience: Ages 7-10
Identifiers: LCCN 2025002180 (print)
LCCN 2025002181 (ebook)
ISBN 9798892138550 (hardcover)
ISBN 9798892138567 (paperback)
ISBN 9798892138574 (ebook)
Subjects: LCSH: Big bang theory—Juvenile literature. Cosmology—Juvenile literature.
Classification: LCC QB991.B54 M33 2026 (print)
LCC QB991.B54 (ebook)
DDC 523.1/8—dc23/eng/20250225
LC record available at https://lccn.loc.gov/2025002180
LC ebook record available at https://lccn.loc.gov/2025002181

Editor: Alyssa Sorenson
Designer: Emma Almgren-Bersie

Photo Credits: Romolo Tavani/Shutterstock, cover; CFH DESIGN/Shutterstock, 1; Oleksandra/Adobe Stock, 3 (asteroids); Stockbym/Adobe Stock, 3 (planet); zhukovvvlad/Shutterstock, 4; JPL-Caltech/NASA, 5 (foreground); Klever_ok/Shutterstock, 5 (background); Stefan Holm/Shutterstock, 6; IkaPhoto/Shutterstock, 7; Adolf Schaller for STScI/NASA, 8-9; NASA, ESA, N. Smith (University of California, Berkeley), and The Hubble Heritage Team (STScI/AURA) Credit for CTIO Image: N. Smith (University of California, Berkeley) and NOAO/AURA/NSF, 10-11; remotevfx/Shutterstock, 12-13; Triff/Shutterstock, 14-15; Outer Space/Shutterstock, 16 (screen); FOTOGRIN/Shutterstock, 16 (monitor); ESA and the Planck Collaboration/JPL/NASA, 17 (screen); Yeti studio/Shutterstock, 17 (monitor); sankai/iStock, 17 (background); Rain Ungert/iStock, 18-19; NASA, ESA, CSA, STScI, Jose M. Diego (IFCA), Jordan C. J. D'Silva (UWA), Anton M. Koekemoer (STScI), Jake Summers (ASU), Rogier Windhorst (ASU), Haojing Yan (University of Missouri), 20-21; brain_fix/Shutterstock, 23.

Printed in the United States of America at Corporate Graphics in North Mankato, Minnesota.

TABLE OF CONTENTS

CHAPTER 1
Our Universe...4

CHAPTER 2
The Beginning...6

CHAPTER 3
Always Growing....................................16

ACTIVITIES & TOOLS
Try This!..22
Glossary..23
Index..24
To Learn More.......................................24

CHAPTER 1
OUR UNIVERSE

Look around you. What do you see? Everything on Earth is part of the **universe**.

Milky Way galaxy

Everything in outer space is, too. The universe is huge. It holds everything, including time! It has billions of **galaxies**. It has countless stars. Planets, **black holes**, and other space objects are part of it, too.

CHAPTER 2
THE BEGINNING

Around 13.8 billion years ago, the universe and everything in it did not exist. Then a single point appeared. It was very **dense**. It was very hot.

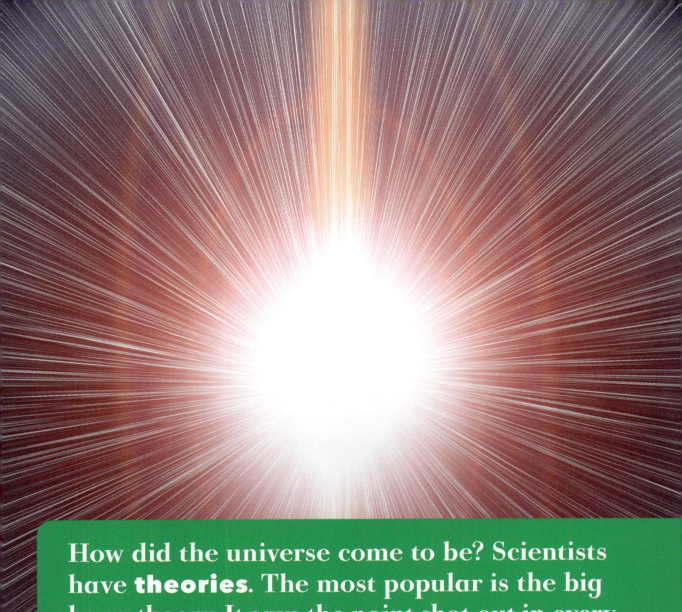

How did the universe come to be? Scientists have **theories**. The most popular is the big bang theory. It says the point shot out in every direction! This took less than one second. It was the big bang. The universe was made. But it looked very different.

CHAPTER 2 7

At first, the universe was very hot. It was about 18 billion degrees Fahrenheit (10 billion degrees Celsius). Then it cooled. **Particles** formed. They combined. They made **elements**, such as the gases hydrogen and helium.

CHAPTER 2

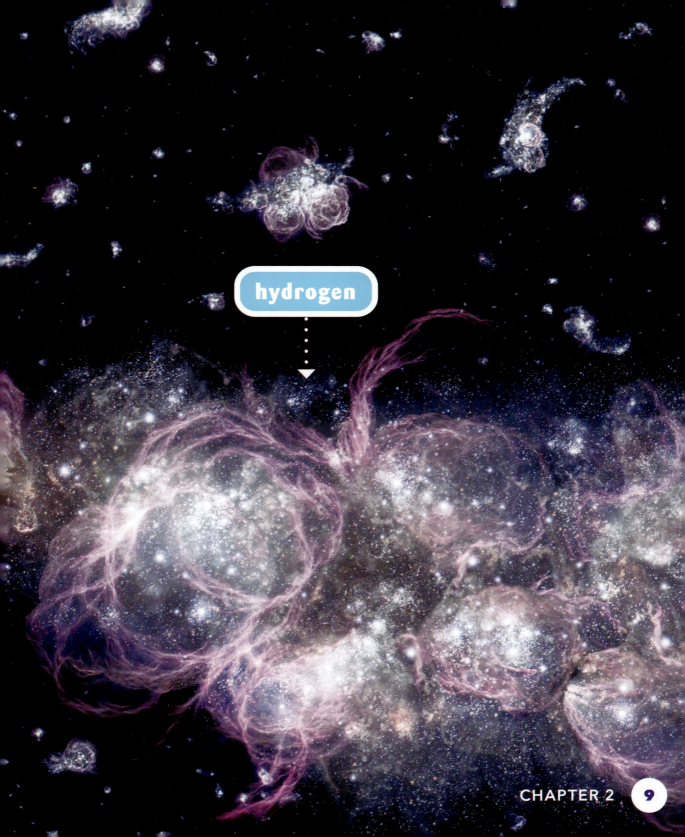

Hydrogen and helium are needed to make stars. But stars did not form right away. Millions of years passed. Clouds of dust and gas floated in space. The clouds were cold. This made gases stick together in clumps.

Some clumps crashed into each other. They combined and grew. Their **gravity** grew stronger, too. They pulled in more **matter**. Eventually, their gravity grew too strong. They fell in on themselves. This made them very hot. They turned into stars.

DID YOU KNOW?

Stars live up to trillions of years. They eventually die. Very large stars explode when they die. This is called a supernova. It can leave behind a black hole.

Areas where these stars formed were called protogalaxies. Protogalaxies moved in space. They crashed into other protogalaxies. They grew into galaxies. The universe as we know it started taking shape!

TAKE A LOOK!

How did the universe take shape? Take a look!

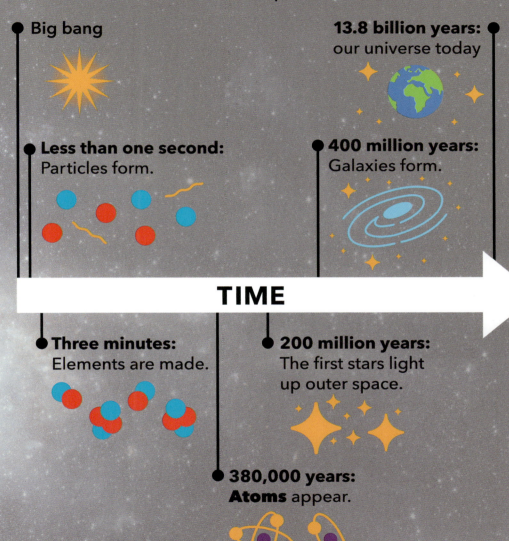

- **Big bang**
- **Less than one second:** Particles form.
- **Three minutes:** Elements are made.
- **380,000 years: Atoms** appear.
- **200 million years:** The first stars light up outer space.
- **400 million years:** Galaxies form.
- **13.8 billion years:** our universe today

TIME

CHAPTER 2

CHAPTER 3

ALWAYS GROWING

The big bang is a theory. There are others. One theory says we are living in a **virtual** world. A computer could be running our universe!

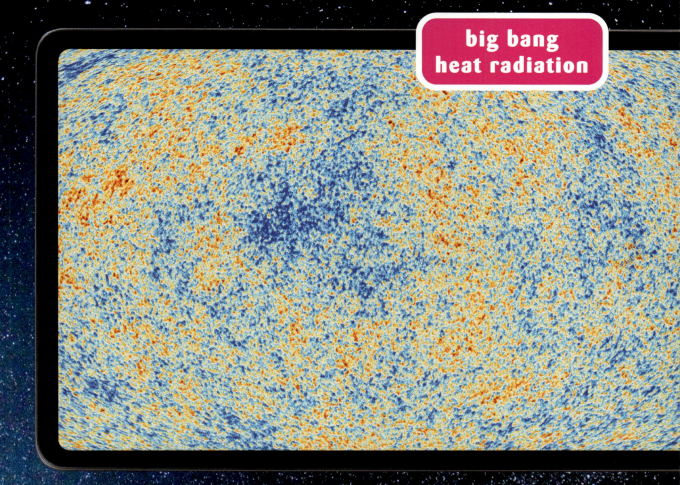

big bang heat radiation

But most scientists believe the big bang theory. Why? **Data** backs it up. The big bang created heat **radiation**. Scientists found it. They were able to make a picture of it.

CHAPTER 3

The universe is huge. Scientists continue to study it. How? They look at very old light. Light travels through space. It comes from space objects like stars. Some stars are billions of **light-years** away. When their light reaches us, we see what those stars looked like billions of years ago.

We cannot see the big bang itself. Why? A thick cloud is in the way. No light shines through. But scientists keep searching. They want more **evidence** to prove the big bang theory.

DID YOU KNOW?

Some scientists think our universe isn't alone. There may be other universes out there!

The universe is still growing. How do we know? Scientists study faraway galaxies. Those galaxies are moving away from us!

We still have many questions. What existed before the big bang? Will we ever be able to see it? What other secrets does our universe hold?

DID YOU KNOW?

Scientists think the universe could keep growing forever.

ACTIVITIES & TOOLS

TRY THIS!

GROWING UNIVERSE

Galaxies are moving apart because the universe is growing. How does that work? Find out with this fun activity!

What You Need:
- balloon
- marker

1. Blow up your balloon a little bit. Pinch the neck so the air stays in. The balloon is your universe.
2. Draw dots on your balloon. Make sure they are spread out. These are your galaxies.
3. Blow up the balloon more. What happens to the galaxies?
4. What does this tell you about our universe?

GLOSSARY

atoms: The tiniest parts of elements that have all the properties of those elements. All matter in the universe is made up of atoms.

black holes: Areas in space where stars have collapsed and where gravity is so strong that nothing can escape, not even light.

data: Information collected so something can be done with it.

dense: Packed together tightly.

elements: Substances that cannot be divided into simpler substances.

evidence: Information and facts that help prove something is true or false.

galaxies: Very large groups of stars and planets.

gravity: The force that pulls things toward the center of a space object and keeps them from floating away.

light-years: Measures of distance in space. One light-year is 5.9 trillion miles (9.5 trillion kilometers).

matter: Something that has weight and takes up space, such as a solid, liquid, or gas.

particles: Extremely small pieces or amounts of something.

radiation: The giving off of energy in the form of light or heat.

theories: Ideas based on some facts or evidence but not proved.

universe: All existing matter and space.

virtual: Made to seem like the real thing but consisting mainly of sound and images.

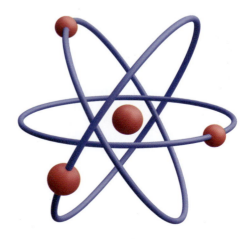

ACTIVITIES & TOOLS   23

INDEX

atoms 15
black holes 5, 12
crashed 12, 14
data 17
dense 6
Earth 4
elements 8, 15
evidence 19
galaxies 5, 14, 15, 20
gravity 12
heat radiation 17
helium 8, 11

hydrogen 8, 11
light-years 19
matter 12
outer space 5, 11, 14, 15, 19
particles 8, 15
planets 5
protogalaxies 14
scientists 7, 17, 19, 20
stars 5, 11, 12, 14, 15, 19
supernova 12
theories 7, 16, 17, 19
virtual world 16

TO LEARN MORE

Finding more information is as easy as 1, 2, 3.
1. Go to www.factsurfer.com
2. Enter "bigbang" into the search box.
3. Choose your book to see a list of websites.

ACTIVITIES & TOOLS